Y0-EKR-445

Learning To Fly

Learning To Fly

Sarah Katreen Hoggatt

Spirit Water Publications
Salem, Oregon

LEARNING TO FLY

Copyright © 2002, 2003, 2010 by Sarah Katreen Hoggatt

Second Edition

SPIRIT WATER PUBLICATIONS
P.O. Box 7522
Salem, Oregon 97303

All rights reserved. No part of this
book may be reproduced in any form
or by any means, without permission
in writing from the publisher.

Library of Congress Control Number: 2010914598

ISBN-13: 978-0-9729460-2-5
ISBN-10: 0-9729460-2-0

Printed and bound by:
Gorham Printing
3718 Mahoney Drive
Centralia, WA 98531

Cover Art by Emily Cahal
Cover Design by Janelle Wheeler Olivarez
Illustrated by Richard McConochie

For additional copies, contact Spirit Water Publications at
www.SpiritWaterPublications.com

Manufactured in the United States of America

Dedication

To the Lord All Powerful,
who is the true writer of this book.
Thank You for giving me my wings and
for teaching me how to fly.
You are my beginning, my end,
and everything I am and ever shall be.
I love You.

Contents

Chapter 4: Bird Song

Chapter 5: Broken Wings

Chapter 6: Flight Lessons

Acknowledgements

When I started putting all of my poetry together, I had no idea it would one day become a book. The journey to this point has held many adventures. At times it has held turbulence and at others, smooth flying. But I have not come this far on my own, God has given me many fellow travelers to help in the work and for that, I have been truly humbled. So this book would not be complete without giving thanks to the community of people who flew along side and supported me on the way.

First I would like to thank my illustrator and friend, Richard McConochie, for all your tireless effort in bringing my poetry to life through your beautiful drawings. Your advice and council have been instrumental in getting this book published and I am glad to say we both did something with our gifts and talents.

To Rebekah Borah, my brilliant graphic artist. Thank you so much for all the effort and time you gave to this project and for the many answers to the questions I peppered you with throughout the writing of both editions. It is invaluable to have you, in whose opinion I hold such trust, beside me as graphic artist and editor. Your knowledge and expertise was just what I needed. You have a deep love for God and a heart to serve His people, for that I will be ever grateful.

To Ryan and Laurie Canney who are the best editors any writer could ask for. Thank you for your enthusiasm for this book, for all of the corrections you made, and for your love for me. I am immeasurably grateful for you both.

To Dolores Dahl whose own books inspired and served as a model for this one. Thank you for all of your expert guidance and support as I put this book together. I don't know where I would be with publishing my writing without your footsteps to follow those many years ago. You unflagging encouragement and loving friendship have enriched my life in so many ways.

To Emily Cahal for giving me the honor of having your photographic art grace this cover and the biography page, and for shocking me with what you can do in Photoshop. You have taught me a great deal about honoring who we are and who we've been; lessons I have relearned while redesigning this book. Thank you for teaching them to me.

To Janelle Wheeler Olivarez who designed the cover so beautifully. It means a great deal to me to have this book redone and I am grateful for the time you gave to be a part of it.

To Hinrich and Laurel Muller who gave of their time and book publishing expertise in the final preparation of this manuscript. Thank you for your hospitality and technical assistance during those final laps to the finish line.

To Jennifer C. Cornell. Your belief in me and the power of my writing has been an inspiration for many years now. I consider myself blessed to have been under your tutelage. You are truly a gift from God.

To Kathie Fruhwirth who has been a friend and teacher ever since I first started writing poetry. Without you and your foresight to save my early work, some of these poems would have been lost long ago. Together, the poetry and I thank you.

To my friends and family. You are such a joy to me and I shall be ever grateful for you. Thank you for always being so supportive of my writing, for your enthusiasm as I have written this book, for being the inspiration behind many of the words within it, and for all the love you have given to me yesterday, today, and always. You are in my prayers and in my heart.

Last but certainly not least, to all the people who have found something worthwhile in my writing and urged me to publish. Not only did many of you believe I could write this book but you bought it before it was even first published. It is because of you that this book and the ones that follow it exists today. Thank you.

Introduction to First Edition

In my head is a picture of a girl sitting alone on the edge of a cliff overlooking the sea. The sun is setting in a blaze of color, but as beautiful as it is, she yearns for more than what she knows. She is longing to fly over the crashing waves, over the endless pulse of sea into the forever of beyond. Her eyes search the horizon for some glimpse of the unknown she has never seen but nothing ever comes.

Then one day as she is hugging her knees to her chest, a Man appears before her and holds out His hand. This Man's grip, so familiar to her heart, is strong and gentle. He takes her around the waist, and holding her close, walks off the cliff into the open air. At first she is afraid because He might let go and nothing would break her fall. But as they fly up into the clouds away from the world, she forgets her fear in the light of His joy and enjoys the view. Together, they soar into a deep blue sky, her arms outstretched, catching the wind and twirling about. He then throws her up into the air, and laughingly, catches her as she falls back down, soon off to explore more expanses of the sky. Like graceful birds they move as one, the Lover and the beloved, ever sealed in an eternal bond. Knowing this, the girl is at peace with going back to earth to tell her story of when she learned to fly until her Lover comes to take her forever home.

Like the girl, I will tell you my story of how I learned to fly, through perils, exultations, tears, healing, and love. For it takes time to step out of the nest, flap our wings, discover the possibilities, and take off. Flying is to see the world from a unique perspective, to wash in the peace that is there in the sky for those of us willing to leave what we know behind, to surrender everything we ever hope to be, and to embrace a wider perspective, to wash in the peace that is there in the sky for those of us willing to leave what we know behind, to surrender everything we ever hope to be, and to embrace a wild love. Learning to fly means far more than experiencing the sensation of weightlessness itself: It's knowing the Teacher Himself and all the delight intimacy with Him can hold; He is worth stepping off the cliff for. In the following pages, I hope the telling of my journey, my flying lessons, will enable you to come to know your own.

Sarah Katreen Hoggatt
Salem, Oregon
October 2002

Introduction to Second Edition

Life is a funny thing. As we walk the road, we can't fully understand where we have come from and we certainly don't know where we are going. All we can do is take the next step in front of us trusting in God to guide us and in our own hearts to hear His truth within. We never see a map, however often we request one, but in time we come to know there is rarely a right path upon which to tread, correct steps for our feet. Instead, we learn that we live in a wide world with vast forests, open fields, and tall cliffs where we can run, laugh, fly, and yes, even struggle.

It has now been eight years since this book was first published and though I have learned a great deal since that time in my faith, in my relationships, and in living, I am touched by the voice of my younger self who still felt there was a path through the woods, correct steps for my feet. While redesigning these pages and adding new material, I have come to hear my younger self in a different way and I now have a new respect for who I was where before I was embarrassed at my struggles and the brokenness I carried. But now I know we need not be ashamed of where we've been. God honors such struggles, He respects our courage in facing those battles and therefore, so should we respect who we've been and where we've walked.

God loves our journeys. He loves watching us run through the fields, climb the trees, and wade in the rivers. In fact, He is right there with us and though the journey may not be a perfect one in our own eyes, it is perfectly beautiful in His.

As I reflect back on the poetry in these pages, some of them ring truer for me now than they did then, some I treasure as memories past, and some stand out as prophecy for the future ahead, lines that became very real for me years down the road and in far deeper ways. Most of these poems were written without any idea of ever publishing them so the feedback I have heard from people who have read this book and found meaning in its pages for their own lives have touched me that much more deeply. That God would take these words, these lines that came from a very open and honest heart—struggles, joys, and all—and use them in the lives of others is a humbling honor that still brings tears to my eyes. Along with God, I can now say I am truly proud of these writings, even more than I was when I first wrote them, and I am proud of the woman from whom they came.

This is the journey we all walk and what I have learned is we can't be ashamed about any of the paths we have taken. We can't hide where we've been, we can only take what we've learned and make new choices with what we now know, explore new places. Who we are and who we have been is not something to run away from, it is something to honor. Every part of ourselves is precious, every inch made by God. If I carry one thing away from my time reworking this book, it is this: It is important to be honest and open about what is real in my heart and to voice those things, for "real and honest" is what God uses to touch the lives of others in ways I can't even imagine.

In all, there are eleven new poems in this book, six new illustrations, and the new cover. It has been a delight to update the book in these ways and to make it a matching companion for the second book that followed three years later, *In His Eyes*. *Learning to Fly* is the beginning of my journey; it is where I am from and where I once dreamed of going. Most of all, it is about the One who still goes with me.

Looking back, I see the "right" path I was walking never even truly existed so it's ironic that this book is about learning to fly, for it is now I realize that while I was trying to walk that path, I was flying before I even knew how.

Sarah Katreen Hoggatt
Salem, Oregon
October 2010

Learning to Fly

Perched
on the Cross

The beginning of all stories,
the end of all tales,
will ever be
the night on Calvary's hill.

Symphony

Waves tumble over each other
in a thundering race to reach the shore.
Sea gulls fly overhead as if to see
which one can sail closest to the water.
The sun sinks low, setting ablaze
fire in the darkening sky as
God stands above, orchestrating
His symphony of nature.

The Dark Hand that Holds You

The sun is shining
　　　　but my heart is full of woe.
This disparity abounds above
as we trifle here below.

This land we tread is troubled,
　　　　but I really don't know why.
The road we walk is crumbling,
but surely we must try.

This transient life
　　　　filled with unseeing eyes,
blindly wandering around
and falling for the lies.

He fills them with delusions
　　　　and hateful evil things.
Making them all believe
the fearful things he brings.

He will grab your neck
　　　　and shake you till you drop,
make you carry guilt and shame
until your spirit stops.

He rejoices in your downfall,
　　　　will haunt you with terror in the night,
brings painful memories to heart,
and cackles at your fright.

He will never care and
       hangs like a shadow overhead.
On this earth he'll never leave you
until your love for God is dead.

He sucks the joy out from you
       and drains your essence all away,
with worries and with emptiness
until in a hollow shell you'll stay.

But the power that he has
       is the greatest when you let
him come into your life
without you knowing yet.

He'll turn and give you a smile,
       put on his Sunday best,
then turn and show his ugly face
and drown you with the rest.

He'll delight to watch you struggle
        as you fight against the pain,
throw the stones of trouble at you
and watch you do it all again.

Making sure you're stricken
        and unable to battle back,
he unmercifully takes your breath away,
and tosses heavy weights upon your back.

He'll savor every heartache
        and make sure you're all alone.
No one there beside you
to hear your lonely moan.

Like wheat from the field,
        he'll thrash you on the floor,
twist you all together,
and crush his will upon you more.

Hating the very thought of you,
        except in the hurting he can do,
separating you from the One who saves,
the One who could see you through.

For He is the one he really hates,
        the one that holds the key,
to life everlasting in Heaven,
and saving grace for you and me.

Do not fear this evil foe,
        for we don't have to fight.
The battle is already won
as we look toward the light.

Death on a Cross

In the dark dreary shadows of
the lowest end of existence,
I stand stripped and wasted of
any dignity I defied to ever have.
Lamenting my beloved's
twisting in cold hate,
I abandon and cast myself away
from the only crags I clung to.
I have not one solaced place
to rest my weary soul.
Only one last act of love to give
and only one note left to sing.
The very best piece of myself have I given,
I have tirelessly spent my whole being and
to you, seemed to crash woefully short.
When every man whether
of sacred fire or burning blood
spurns my howling cries,
When the rancorous lashes
are rendered never ending,
ripping into ragged remnants
my repudiated self.
When I am destroyed among the
crashing bellows of the death-black sea and
torn to unrecognizable shards
of filth by flesh hungry demons,
having been discarded, condemned,
to die a death alone and
deploringly stripped of any
dross dream you may have had for me,
only then, you shall be redeemed
and I shall guide you home.

Peter's Soliloquy

I'm standing in front of a sea of faces,
    my Lord's words ring in my head.
    Images haunt my inner spirit,
and now my Savior is dead.

He lovingly called me forth,
    I was inexperienced and He knew,
    I would follow Him for all to see,
but I would betray Him too.

With just one word, one single look,
    He could touch the deepest place in my soul.
    I longed to be near the lamp of life,
purged by the fire, this man who made me whole.

As I wander alone through the streets,
    ghostly voices tugging at my heart.
    Finally knowing how cruel this is,
for it's tearing my world apart.

Judas' Lament

I am falling in nothingness.
No way to save myself, no way to stop.
My soul is tortured, my dreams condemned.
The flesh on my body is torn to shreds.
I find no peace, the darkness closes in around me.
Drowning, water rises, filling my lungs.
No will to live, I flow with the current;
one tear, frozen on my cheek for all
time to tell of my sharp inner pain.
My mangled self is no longer there,
only an empty soul crying out in pure misery.
Hidden from the world,
I am alone with this wretched existence.
Oh, how I long to die!
Sweet Jesus, take this bitter life from me,
take me down.
Cut my heart out and cast me out to burn in hell.
Anything but these cruel chains,
for I am held in bondage.
To die is the sweetest thing of all.
Flowing blood is flowing honey to my sight.
Death can be the only escape for me now.
I want to throw myself at Your feet
and weep to the sky.
Dear God, I beg of You to kill me,
I can no longer live.
Searing pain overwhelms me and takes control.
I am laid helpless at the devil's gate.
Save me and take me to You dear Jesus.
Only in You I find my rest, take me to Your side.

Winding Rings

Wreaths adorned the window panes,
hanging with a red ribbons flare.
Garland swinging high and low
to wrap us in a warm embrace.
Now ever the green has been turned to
the white lily's bloom.
Cascading down from the empty cross,
standing tall, open to us all.
They welcome the new dawn,
the dawn of a new age and a new eternity.
Our forever life, yet entirely His.
The circle winds around in this
ever lasting out flowing of love and life.

Learning to Fly

A Life for My Lord and Savior

Grief in His eyes and tears on my cheek.
Faith, love, peace, and compassion,
all have been destroyed.
There is nothing left.
All sense of living is gone.
A life without love is not life at all.
Blood streaming down His body,
His eyes focused up to the heavens.
Innocent but with everything to die for,
birds no longer sing as
rocks are thrown one by one.
Bruises on His body and tears in His eyes.
He did not deserve death,
He deserved to be praised.
Miracles and love have now ceased to exist.
Listen, my Lord talks up to Heaven!
See His spirit of fire leaving the people.
Forever gone like light blown from a candle
but always able to return
if I can just light the match.
See His body carried into the tomb.
Perfume and oils cannot hide
what has happened on this fateful day.
Go to the tomb, see the angels, embrace the light.
My Lord and Savior, risen from the dead!
I can no longer be condemned
to the patterns of this world.
I must live the life I was born to live,
a life for my Lord and Savior.

Heavenly Wonder

I wonder what it will be like
      to hear the angels sing,
and I wonder what I'll feel
      when the bells of His glory ring?

What a glorious appearing
      when I shall see His face,
and what tears of joy shall overcome
      when I bow and take my place.

I know when I shall enter
      I'll fall down upon my knees,
and cry, "Holy, holy and hosanna!"
      like Joseph's eleven sheaves.

What awe and grateful tremblings
      shall overtake me then,
and what a sense of wonder
      when I fully understand amen.

But for now I'll dream and try to see
      this vision far away,
which is really around the corner,
      so I will live for You today.

Flying in Unison

*The gift of a friend
shall ever priceless be
an eternal bond between two,
loving and free.*

Friend

Some people go through life
wondering where to go.
Other people go through life
not knowing they're supposed to go anywhere at all.
I'm glad I know someone who knew exactly
where to go.
Up a hill and to a cross.
The Lord has given me many things,
but one of my favorites is a simple six letter word,
friend.
A friend is someone who knows you
and loves you just the same.
Someone who has an open ear for you
or a shoulder to lean on.
A person who is willing to open up
their heart to you.
I thank God that doesn't
even come close to who you are.
I thank Him that He has let me know such
a wonderful, caring, and beautiful person,
and that I have the privilege
of calling you my friend.

Flying in Unison

Beloved

My beloved friends,
more beauty has not been told.
With sparkling eyes and brilliant smiles,
giving hearts, lovelier than gold.
In one moment, I wonder how you know
what the touch of a friend can do,
the acceptance it can show.
I can't comprehend, but hope I will see,
why you do understand,
my beloved friends,
so precious and dear to me.

Skating

Swung around like the end of a rope,
　my hands clasped in yours.
　　You're every part of my breath and being.
　　Watching you across the ring, joy fills my heart.
　　My blinded eyes never saw true wealth.
　　Skating across the floor,
　　palm outstretched, I know you're there.
　　Without looking, your presence glides beside me.
　Our wall of faith held as one,
and I am alive, I have you.

Hands

You have ageless hands,
hurt and joy intertwined.
Hands that have bled,
capable hands.
Belonging to you and yet,
the manifestation of another time,
another river of pain.
Hands that survive,
your hands.

For the Love of a Father

As God reigns above,
we walk the trail of life.
Fleeting moments fade
into the dark of night while
love shared between two
shines in the cosmos.
With colors parading forth,
the constant cords of strength
are held tight around us.
They do not fray or tear
but are a constant pull
bringing us forth into
the arms of a King.
His face is a vision before our eyes
as together we journey to His heart.
With you I walk this path,
not because of convenience or even joy,
but because He has bound us together
in an eternal home.
The knot our Father has shaped
will not lose its hold.
It stays through thunder and heat,
through both anguish and glory.
His promises to us are etched in
the stones He holds in His hands,
promises that will never be broken.
And it is because of this everlasting love,
we know what He has cared for and built
between us will never be taken.
It is because of Him,
I can share with you my heart,
the knowledge I will love you

despite of events within and around us.
For this gift is real,
perhaps the most real thing
we will ever know.
The love of a Father
shared between two.

Forever to Be

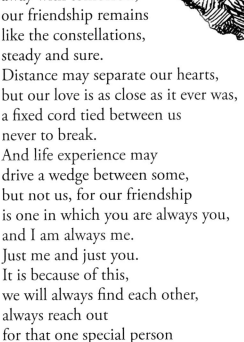

Though time may sail
throughout our lives
taking our yesterdays
away with tomorrow,
our friendship remains
like the constellations,
steady and sure.
Distance may separate our hearts,
but our love is as close as it ever was,
a fixed cord tied between us
never to break.
And life experience may
drive a wedge between some,
but not us, for our friendship
is one in which you are always you,
and I am always me.
Just me and just you.
It is because of this,
we will always find each other,
always reach out
for that one special person
who will stand by our side
no matter what comes.
Forever and ever to be,
that's you and me.

Life Force

I remember when I was with you my friend.
You taught me about life and
how to fly in the scarlet sky.
Like to a garden full of beauty and light we came.
I have imagined castles in the morning,
and you singing to me in the evenings.
Together, there is a reflected flame of depth,
a shining essence of which we still pour out and drink.
Immense music filled the moment,
capturing me in grace.
Expressions of my love
illustrate what is real and true.
And when I'm with you, it's like a gorgeous song.
My love is a harmony,
a fiery sea full of silhouetted dreams.
Watch me wishing for the inspired night I had found,
the crystal eves I knew.
For a friend like you is true magic
and a light to my life.

Brightest Blessings

Beautiful child,
gentle touch soul,
strong fighting spirit,
dancing, heart full.

Pure through the fire,
brilliantly bright,
blessing from birth,
God-given light.

Priceless Treasure

Do you know what you have given me?
In a time of turbulence and change,
you have shown me love.
You want me walking among you
and I now belong within your walls and
in your arms of compassion.
I am deeply moved by your sincerity
and your thoughtfulness.
What a glorious gift,
what a precious, priceless treasure
God has given me in you.
I thank you with all that I am for
welcoming me into your family
and know that I will serve you and
love you with all of my heart.

A Psalm of Thanks

I have watched you seek the Lord
and thus have come to know,
the love shining out from within your eyes,
and the King you're living for.
You have the kind of spirit,
that glows in darkest night,
who sings despite the storm
as you reflect His light.
Should I, a fellow traveler,
be so blessed as to enjoy
the breath of God I see in you
and to learn from you this joy?
What miracle of blessing,
God has chosen I should grow,
to make pure my heart by what you do
and the gracefulness you show.
What a day on journey's end,
when we enter Heaven's door,
when I shall come to find you,
on Heaven's celestial shore.
And on that morning by the sea,
walking hand in hand,
I'll explain how you touched my life,
so you'll finally understand.
Then I hope you'll be blessed to know,
God's changed through you a life.
How He has worked through you,
teaching love through strife.
So thank you now for all you are,
and for the beauty of your soul.

Learning to Fly

Thank you for the life you gave
to God who made us whole.
For I am better because of you,
I'm closer to his heart,
dreaming of the day when I can
thank you for your part.

Children of God

Breath of an angel,
whisper of wings,
bright from above,
mystically sings.
Humming a tune,
brush of a breeze,
humbles a heart
down on its knees.
Blessings of beauty,
gifts full of grace,
God's holy children
reflect His Son's face.

Seen Through Another's Eyes

The tree of life grows larger leaves,
    weaving sights the eye perceives,

as if to stand on ocean's shore,
    noticing things you never have before.

Rings of wonder round your mind,
    reflections of your soul to find.

Things you never thought you'd do,
    archaic lands transformed to new.

The world still holds intense surprise
    when you see through another's eyes.

Flowers Never Die

There is a bounty upon this earth
of blooms we'll never know,
and though we've heard of hints of them,
    there are no flowers in winter snow.
We may have heard their voices,
seen their stems and petals dear,
but they were gone before we knew them,
    we never knew them here.
But there is a day in Heaven,
when God'll give us each bouquets,
flowers of ones we barely knew,
    in eternity's brighter blaze.

Learning to Fly

Building Strength

Building strength in my wings,
discovering who I am inside,
exploring the gifts I have
beside my Heavenly Guide.

Who Am I?

I am a pale pink ribbon withering in the leaves.
I am a flowing river, gurgling over the rocks.
I am a majestic mountain reaching for the sky.
I am who I am; I'm me.

I Can Do Anything

Give me peace, give me love, and give me courage.
With peace I'm calm enough
to make the right decisions.
With love I'll always have someone to back me up.
With courage I know I can do anything I want to do.
With these three things I can move mountains.

The Gift

A while back I received
a beautiful gift simply
because I was special.
I played with it for a time,
then packed it away for I
was too busy for such things.
Now I lift the lid, blow
away the dust, and see it
for all it is worth for I have
come back to myself and
fallen at the feet of the giver.

Learning to Fly

Painting Life

If I could paint a picture,
of what I think and feel,
I would sail it on the ocean
to the foreverness of You.
I would paint with brightest colors,
and deepest shades of hue,
layers of being for Your children
to discover and explore.
I would color a tear and a smile,
hidden in a flaming heart,
and a grove of trees
to symbolize the sanctuary
of spending time with You.
I would paint a river to
tell the lessons I have learned
and a castle on a cliff so
we could walk around my dreams.
There would be a winding path of healing,
from the broken rocks below,
and a bird soaring on lifted wing
calling out its sacred song.
I would paint the gift of friendship,
two joining hands as one,
and shining lights out in the sky
to illustrate all the blessings from above.
But the diamond of it all,
is I would show Your love,
an ever moving circle,
the eternal joy of two.
I would paint this life force,
the greatest gift I know,
so then they all would see
what I painted for.

Soul Fire

How can I ever express
what is burning inside?
A hot fire raging within me,
held in check until its time.
Standing before a sea wreathed in flames,
crimson waves burning around my feet.
Like a dam of boiling water
about to break free,
I run along the edge,
the rocks already cracking
under my anxious pace.
As the foundation comes apart,
I fall into the burning flood,
lost to myself in the flames of the soul.

Tiger

I write because it's a part of me.
It wanders around inside,
poking the insides of the cage,
building to its release.
Like a trapped tiger,
it paces forward and back,
its eyes frozen on my transfixed face,
biding its time till expression.
Then the door's bolt has been torn open
and... POUNCE!
The tiger is all that remains.

A Feast of the Spirit

My whole being is a tool,
swirling in the turbulent fire.
Overwhelming power swells up inside,
I don't understand it and I can't comprehend.
I ask myself if I'm strong enough to be weak,
to become an instrument of God.
What I write takes a hold of me
and flows out of my soul.
I have an extraordinary talent and it mystifies me.
The words take control and dance upon my heart.
I underestimate my own work
and it continues to amaze me at what it can do.
Creation takes flight, grabs me and soars.
I see the deep fathom of my mind yet know it not,
it lies in shadow, veiled and unclear.
I hold this gift in the palm of my hand
and gaze in wonderment.
My own creation has captured me,
not in chains but in silent bondage.
My voice cannot be silenced,
I must speak out.
To not send out the fruit of
my imagination is
to starve.
I cannot wither
or fade away,
I must feast whatever my
future may be.
So I stretch out my
hand for it shall lead
me home.

Voice of the Tide

Beyond the burst of birds,
flowing pure and wide,
your voice I sense within me—
words reverberating through my head,
thunder churning on the sea,
the pulse of waves,
steady and strong,
calling me—
to face into the dawn—
to see the world anew—
beyond the endless shore.

The Wanderers

They are the wanderers,
the faces without a home.
They are the hopeful,
for a better time yet to come.
They are the trapped ones,
trying to see visions through worldly bars.
They are the ones we see,
but don't know.
The ones we love,
but can't protect.
They are everywhere,
looking for somewhere,
knowing that tomorrow,
may find them anywhere at all.
These are the wanders,
a vast army of yet to be,
and I am one of them.

Learning to Fly

When We Danced

I don't remember the moment,
the time when we first met,
when you looked into my eyes
          of your baby, Heaven sent.
And I confess, I don't recall
you watching as I sleep,
cuddled close in blankets tight,
          down in dreamland deep.
I'm sorry to say it's left my mind,
my very first day of school,
because I'm sure as you watched me go
          your heart of pride was full.
I dearly wish I could recollect
the love you felt inside
at all the times I was hurt and fell
          and I ran to you and cried.
But I realize I will never know
the light inside your soul
as you saw me doing things myself
          and released me to God's control.
But the one thing I remember,
the moment that entranced,
was the night when we joined our hands,
          released ourselves and danced.
For it was that precious moment
of your delight in me,
my favorite memory wrapped in love
          for all eternity.
Then like you, there will come a time
when I have newborn eyes to see,
and I will dance with her
          like I danced with thee.

Spirit of My People

Drums beating as flames dance high,
father eagle soaring on lifted wings.
Moccasined feet gliding though the forest
beside the breathing waters of lady river.
Chants ring, echoing in the air,
calling me to the wild spirit bestowed upon me.
Sweeping me up into the hallowed dance on
New Moons Eve, feet pound the earth in
perfect synch with the beat of my blood.
As my spirit holds communion with
those who have gone before me,
I am called back to the age of my heart,
back to the arms of my people and my land.

Bird Song

I will praise You to the heavens,
I will shout with the earth,
running to You,
the King of new birth.

Come

Come, You say.
I don't want to come.
I am fine where I am, I'm comfortable.
But You insist, why do You insist so fiercely?
I don't know what's over there, it's strange.
I won't know what to do and I'm scared.
Why do You care what I do?
Why do You want me to come over there?
What do You want of me?
I don't care who You are, I'm not coming.
Still You persist, come.
Listen to me! I'm staying here.
No, I don't care if You'll give me the strength.
I don't lean on anybody, not You and not them.
I don't need Your love, love is a waste of time.
Come.
Do I want the truth? Doesn't everybody?
Isn't everybody searching for something?
What am I searching for?
That's none of Your business!
You already know? How could You know?
Lucky guess. But how could You know that?
I've never told anyone. You know me completely?
Yeah, right. I don't even really know myself.
Come. But why?
Do I trust You? I don't know.
You love me? No one has loved me like that.
Not that much.
Come. You'll be with me?
Why would You stay with someone like me?
I don't understand You.
Why can't You let me stay here? I'm happy here.

Do I want to grow? I'm tall enough.
Oh, You mean like that.
It's beyond my imagination?
I'll admit, that's enticing.
Why do You say I am finished here?
You say there is more for me than this? How?
Just come.
Do You promise You will never leave my side?
Are You sure You will never leave me?
All right, keep me close Lord, I'll come.

Golden Cord

I've seen the gift of miracles
in the blackened foggy night.
I've seen the gift of wonder
in Your frightening glory light.

And You have seen me stumble
for what I want today,
and You have seen me running
away from what You say.

Then I feel the showers
of Your flowing mercy, Lord,
and You teach me how to follow You,
this, the golden cord.

But the beauty of it all
is the love You've given free,
so the children whom You treasure
will Your blessings be.

Revolving Doors

Dear Lord, I know You're out there
listening to every plea,
but Lord I just have one concern
and I'm sorry to say it's me.
You saw how much I sinned today
and went against Your will,
You know how much my heart hurts,
for it is fighting still.
I tried to make the right decisions
but with temptation I went astray.
I didn't take time to talk with You
and so went the other way.
I want to say I'm sorry
and to confess away my sin,
but my pride tells me to hide it
and oftentimes it wins.
It seems to be a struggle,
a pull for You then me,
a fight with my old self
and You who sets me free.
So please destroy the one I was
and place in me a heart
of Your eternal beauty
so from You I'll never part.
I am ready to be sacrificed
wholly unto You,
guide me away from all my sin
so I can live anew.

Dancing

Father, I've had a vision full of wonder and joy.
You and I were dancing on the clouds
with a deep blue sky overhead and I was in
Your arms in a world all our own.
You held me close, kissed me on the face and smiled.
Calling out my name, Your eyes were gleaming
and the beauty of Your face was all I could see.
As the universe fell away, You took my hand,
and held together, led me to the floor.
I began like a child dancing on her daddy's feet.
Held up in Your strong grasp,
I moved my feet trying to copy You.
I saw You watching me while
I tried to cover my mistakes.
Tears streamed, I wanted to get it right.
But Your hands lifted my face and I saw
unshakable love in Your eyes.
I reached out my hand and held fast to Yours
for Your grasp was sure and strong.
Following Your lead, You swung me around,
leaving all I knew behind.
You were all I needed and I smiled at Your pull.
Your timing was perfect and Your voice was sweet.
I felt completely dependent on You, but I thought
I knew the steps, and I stepped out of Your lead.
My heart cried out and I called my
questions to the heavens.
Stripped and cold, I fell to my knees
and wept as the storm raged around me.
Through the rain I heard
You running and I looked up
to see Your arms outstretched with

tears in *Your* eyes.
Longing to hold me,
You swept me up into Your arms
as I cried against Your shoulder.
Holding me safe and secure You soothed me while moving
around the floor as
a mother soothes her child.
In Your embrace I found comfort and tenderness.
Held in Your arms was the only place I wanted
to be for while the world thought I was alone,
they did not see You were carrying me
every step of the dance.
Knowing You were there gave me great peace.
The joy of the glory of the Lord filled my being
and I overflowed with gladness and celebration!
Triumph in You moved my feet as we twirled
together among the clouds and across the sky.
I gazed into the heavens as
tears of joy came over me.
You were looking at me,
grinning, and You held me close.
And now I am longing for the day when
we shall meet for the first time.
Homesick and yearning, I know You too,
are dreaming of me and how You shall come
to claim me as Your own.
I'll look up and see You there and then
we'll run toward each other, rejoicing in our love.
In Your embrace, You will kiss my face
and I will kiss Your feet.
Then You will once again take my hand,
lead me into the heavens,
and together, we'll dance.

Trusting God

Lord, I cry out to You in deep pain.
My soul is lost and alone, scared and shaking.
Your people have cursed me,
my friends have turned away.
Even the ground has been ripped
out beneath my stability.
Outside, I hide behind a mask, happy and free of care, but
inside I'm weeping a sufferer's prayer.

Jesus, the truth is cold, I'm falling fast.
My heart has been broken, bleeding, gaping wide.
The storms of my life have torn me apart and
I am haunted by dark shadows of all that has been.
Silent tears and secret scars
form an everlasting ache.
But my Lord, my God,
please Your child, do not forsake.

Abba, like shattered glass my dreams are in pieces.
I myself have been hurt and have nowhere to go.
You are my love, my life,
don't You care if I am suffering?
Darkness closes in around me,
I am so far from home.
Separated from the light, in a night dark and full,
trapped in the bleakest state, I stare into cold eternal.

Rabbi, part of me says to leave You,
but to whom would I go?
If I looked for the ages,
never would I find such a life as You give.

The deepest part of my being cries
out to You as You are its very essence.
Being taken from You would put to death
the sole source of my being.
I look to You Father, I am laid helpless at Your feet.
Bring me close to You, wrap me in Your arms,
make my peace complete.

Shepherd, give me the joy
like no other I have ever known.
Show me the path to walk,
help me to turn the other cheek.
When I am distressed,
remind me that it is through these times
I shall shed my impurities,
molding me to a closer likeness of You.
Give me the strength to become Your tool in the fire,
to remember You're in control,
to yield, as Your will shall desire.

My Adonai, even through the
difficult times You are there.
You have not left, but carry me
through my times of suffering.
Let trust and praise fill my spirit
as it will bring us closer together.
I will follow wherever You go,
for only in You will I find everlasting love.
Even if I am called a fool by those I care for,
and worldly security falls through the floor,
it can't keep me away from the one true God
now and forevermore.

Wanderlust

My heart yearns for the open road,
new places and awe inspiring sights.
The thrill of new experiences,
exploring distant shores.
Yet my heart is tied and bound,
I have been cinched onto an everlasting tree.
Not the tree I would have chosen,
but fruitful just the same.
Lord, I need direction,
please quiet my sojourned heart with Your fire.
Tell me what to do and give me Your peace
for I feel so torn between the traveled roads
and I'm longing to go home.

Grief and Grace

Father, I am sad and broken.
My dreams are crushed and
what I longed for will not be.
The road I travel is rough,
its ways are treacherous
and the light is dim.
I know not which way to go
and I think it would be easier
if You took me home now.
Could it not be better in Heaven?
I want to leave the world for
I find little hope within its sphere.
Little that I am and little I can do
for Father, I am only one.
What use can I be?
Yet I awake breathing and
You give me the longing to live.
You provide strength to take the next step
and walk with me along the way.
If I live I have purpose.
You have vision for my heart and
love for Your child.
You want me to walk,
You ask me to wait,
to keep hoping to see what
is around the next turn.
You know my anxious heart Father,
my confusion and my shame.
But You, author of all that is good,
will clothe me in Your glory
and I will live by Your grace.

Forever Loved

I stumble toward You
drained and empty of strength.
You pick me up into Your arms
and settle me down in Your love.
Safe in Your protection,
I lay down my heavy head
as You cover me with Your hands.
You are my comfort and my joy.
In You, I will be forever loved.

In Abba's Embrace

In a world of confusion and uncertainty,
You are the only constant thing I have.
I think of my future, it looks so vague and cold
and I feel so lost and disoriented I want to cry.
So I run to You and reach out my hands.
You lift me up into Your embrace and
hold me close to Your chest where
I can feel Your heart beat with love for me.
With Your arms wrapped tightly around my body,
I lay my head on Your shoulder and
my arms cling desperately to Your neck.
You hum a gentle soothing melody while
rocking me back and forth,
tenderly rubbing my back.
As I look into Your face,
a tear rolls down my cheek
and You gently kiss it away.
At last feeling safe and protected,

I am now held in Your embrace,
free to release all that is held inside.
You let me cry away my sorrow-laden troubles,
sobbing out the pain, loneliness, and disappointment.
I weep it all until I have nothing left to cry,
revealing everything that has ached in my heart.
You take it in upon Yourself,
closely listening to what I have to tell.
When I am at last drained and exhausted,
You look at me with loving eyes,
pouring over me with deep compassion as my
eyes grow weary and
my body slowly goes limp in Your arms.
You affectionately touch my face
and caress my cheeks.
Gently, I feel Your hand laid over my heart
as You pull me close, wrapping me up into You and
enveloping me in Your grace and forgiveness.
Inexpressible peace begins to
fill the emptiness of my soul
and unfathomable love washes away all of my pain.
As I fall asleep, softly lulled by Your presence,
I can hear Your sweet, strong voice calling out,
"It is finished."

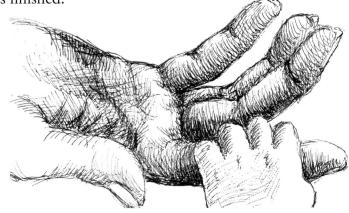

Bird Song

Parakletos

I see you my child.
I see you feeling alone and frightened
as you remember what has gone before.
I feel you shaking, so vulnerable,
and I know the aching of your heart
for what was and for what could have been.
I understand your tears when you cry
and I hurt at the pains you bear.
And the fear? I know that too.
I know how you would just rather forget
the things we've been through.
How you would rather cast in the sea
memories of broken glass and darker skies.
But child, my beloved child,
let Me tell you of another love,
another way of life, my love and my life.
For I will never hurt you and
my touches are gentle and kind.
I walk along beside you holding you up
so you may stand unashamed and strong.
My hand will enclasp yours and
you will find peace within my arms.
I will protect you, you'll be safe and secure.
You no longer need to be afraid, ruled in fear.
Be bold in Me, fear no evil.
Together we will heal the scars and
together we will know true love and true life.
In Me, I will set you free.

The Song That's in My Heart

Lord I'm trying to sing
the song You gave,
the song that's in my heart.
But the world is so confusing,
and I only see a part.
Oftentimes along this
question pitted path
it's all that I can do,
to reach out to grab Your hand
and hold closely onto You.
Sometimes I feel as if
we're dancing across
the clear blue sky,
soaring through the heavens
and bringing Your kingdom nigh.
But at other times
You know, my Lord,
I'm crying at Your feet,
and You have to pick me up
so Your eyes I can meet.
I'm struggling to find
this love plan
You designed.
For my heart is longing to follow
after You in kind.
So now I'm coming to Your
throne to ask for
guidance on my way,
and to plead You for Your presence
that by my side You'll always stay.
I know it's a lot

to ask the Creator
of earth it's true,
but You have said You love me,
and I know that I love You.
So Lord, I'm just
Your precious child
coming with a prayer,
but I can feel You in my heart
so I know You're living there.
Please take me up
into Your arms and
bring me where I should go,
so that way when I die,
I'll see Your face and know.
And if the day shall ever come
when I no longer sing
this beautiful song You gave,
please tell the ones I know and love
that You are God and save.
Amen.

Learning to Fly

One Step More

The hill is so steep and long.
Each step brings us closer to the top,
but the top is so distant and far away.
I feel ready to drop off to the side,
but a voice calls me onward,
"One step more, one step more.
You don't know what's around the bend,
but I'll give you strength for one step more."

Thank You Lord

Thank You Lord
for the gift of Your light
in the eyes of Your children,
shining so bright.

Thank You, Oh Lord,
for holding our hands.
For comfort and strength
because You understand.

Thank You our Lord
for healing our hearts.
For recreating us whole
and giving new starts.

Thank You my Lord
for saving our souls.
United to You,
as love's thunder rolls.

The One

You are the one, Father,
the one who loves me.
The one who understands me
even better than I understand myself.
You are the one who guides me in all my ways
and sits patiently beside me
as I struggle to comprehend.
Out of everyone I know,
You are the only one I depend on.
My lover, my Savior, and precious friend,
it is You alone I hold to.
It is Your lap I climb into
when discouragement aches in my heart.
You are the one who gave up Your life
so You can be with me for eternity.
Your arms are the ones I'm longing for
and it's Your face I'm yearning to see.
You are the one who comforts me in sorrow
and counsels me in confusion.
You are the one I rejoice with and
the more I follow after You,
the more we together, will be one.

A Living Sacrifice

Lord, breathe through me
that I may rely upon Your strength.
Give me Your peace of mind
that I may find hope and joy and
to not be brought down in spirits by daily life.
Help me to realize there is a greater plan,
a greater love than mine.
Give me the awareness of Your presence,
whisper to me with Your still calm voice.
Purify me with fire
so I may have a servant's heart and
help me not to curse or lament the fire,
but to welcome it knowing it's to set me free
of all the ties that hold me away from You.

Never let me leave You Lord,
for I know in my deepest self
a life without You would be worth nothing.
I would be as a stick tossed about
in the waves of a dark and stormy sea.
Keep Yourself foremost in my thoughts, oh Lord,
cover my eyes so I may learn to trust where You lead
even though my own spirit may cry against it.
Fill me with an unwavering faith
and the courage to speak of You freely.
Wrap me in Your presence Lord,
protect me from thoughts that are unpleasing to You.
Be my rock on which I stand
for it is the only place I ever want to be.

I am completely and totally dependent on You Lord.
Take away my fear and help me
to trust You and to know

an ending is really a beginning waiting to start.
Give me the love for Your people
You hold in Your heart
and the fearlessness of trusting You
while tossed in the storm.
Help others to see Your light through me so they
may turn to You and give glory to Your name.

I am but a creation, You are the Creator.
You are the Beginning and the End,
I am but a small speck.
But You call me Your child, the child of Jehovah.
With wonder welling up
and streaming from my heart,
I am in amazed awe over
how much You must love me
to put Your own son to death instead of me.
You give me faith to run the race and strength
to make the leap at just the right time.
As I tumble down, Your arms are there
to catch me and hold me close.

If You were a perfume,
I would soak in You every day.
If You were a friend, I would be forever at Your door.
If You were a fire, I would lie in the
burning embers unwilling to rise.
If You were the sea, I would jump from the cliff.
You are all these things and more.
You paint the earth for Your children
with stars in Your eyes.
I see the sun on the clouds,
the bud of a flower, the light on the grass.
It takes my breath away, and I hear You whisper,
"See how much I love you."

Lord, be forever at my side,
do not leave Your beloved for
I would be utterly lost without You.
You are the one rope
I cling to above the fiery furnace.
You are the air I breathe, the beat of my heart,
You are the light of my world.
May my life be given to You and those You love
like water cascading over into a waterfall,
falling from the heights,
hitting the rocks, yet flowing together unbroken.
May I be an encouragement to others and
may You touch their lives through my words
and what I do. My whole being I give unto You.

Lord, bring me where You know I should go.
Thank You for the angels in my life and
help me to be an angel for others.
I dedicate myself to You Lord,
for there is no greater love and wonder
than what I have found in Your heart.
Lead me, Oh Lord, and never let me leave You
for I love You as I love no other
now and forevermore.

Bird Song

Rags to Riches

Jesus, I am filled with
an overwhelming love for You.
Compared to You Prince of Peace, I am a beggar,
for You own everything there is and I own nothing.
What can I possibly give You to show my devotion?
What do I have You could use for Your kingdom?
I have two arms for hugging,
smiles to pass along good cheer,
and fingers to play music in honor of You.
I can give You a tender heart for loving,
everlasting joy to thank You with,
and a mind to think of other's needs.
I can yield a pair of hands to help in the work,
an uplifted voice to sing Your praises,
and words to encourage and strengthen
the people around me.
I have a pair of knees to help me
bow down before You,
a pair of feet to seek out the ones You love,
and tears to cry in knowing Your children's pain.
I can give my eyes to see Your miracles,
my lips to help me kiss Your feet,
and abounding faith to let You renew my life with.
Jesus, You have made me one of the
richest people in the world, for what do I have?
A life to sacrifice wholly unto You.

Cherries

Abba, knowing You is like
enjoying a large ice-cream sundae
with nuts, whipped cream, chocolate fudge,
and brightly colored sprinkles
on a warm blue-sky day.
Your blessings are like
a bright red cherry on top.
My Father, I want to thank You
for the cherries on my sundae
for You have given me so many they
are cascading over the sides
and falling into the sundaes of others.
Grant that I may always be a cherry
on other people's sundaes and
that when they see my sundae,
they will think of You.

Circle of Prayer

Two heads are bowed
and hands are clasped as one,
searching together
for the love of the Son.

Hearts stand united,
concerns shared between three,
a circle of love
to bind up the free.

Spirits entwining,
gratefulness known,
praising the Father
in heavenly tones.

Growing in love,
turning from sin,
entering His presence,
His peace flowing in.

Drawing them closer
to a heavenly land,
deeper in faith,
resting in God's gentle hand.

Gifts of Today

So often Lord
I become so
caught up in
the concerns of
tomorrow, I miss
many of the
gifts of today.
You have always been
there holding
them out yet I
hardly give them
a second glance
or hold them to
delight in the
treasures they are
much less be
grateful for them.
Help me to stop,
to notice, to say
once again,
"Thank you for
the gifts of today."

I am Forever Yours

Oh Lord, You are the ruler of all things,
there is nothing You don't control.
The roar of the waves, the song of the wind,
and the chirping of the birds all are in Your hands.
Everything I see and think You know full well.
My understanding is limited;
I can't comprehend Your love and greatness
but I am written in the palm of Your hand.
You give me a seat by Your side
so I may be near You.
My master and my friend
shows great compassion.
The wonderful things You have
in store for me are as precious as gold.
You hold me fast in Your arms and
carry me when I cannot stand.
I place my life at Your feet and
cover my eyes with Your spirit.
You lead me with a whisper,
my heart is yearning for You.
The decisions are Yours,
You fight my battle already won.
I fall at Your feet, praise flowing from my lips
and joy from my soul;
I am forever yours.

Ever Thankful

Tears roll down my cheeks
as I fall to my knees in
honor and thanksgiving to You.
You have given me joy
beyond my wildest dreams.
Love overflowing,
setting me free.
Your thunder has rolled,
stilling my ever-quaking heart.
I've stood in amazement as
Your lightening sets the sky ablaze,
lighting up the dark corners of my soul.
I can only watch in wonder as
cascading waves of Your mercy
flows through my life and
washes the old ways away.
Everything is new and fresh
with the evidence of Your touch.
I will trust You forever in eternity
knowing it is in You I am saved.
I look at the life I live,
the love and strength marking each day.
It stuns me to think You could care for me
to set me in such a beautiful creation.
Thankfulness is ever on my lips.
I give You all I have,
a servant's heart seeking after You.
I pray You use it for Your glory.
Brimming with gratefulness for
setting me free by Your grace,
at the end of each day,

I pray with love for the faces before me
and I think with a full heart,
all this and Jesus too?
Thank You Lord God for not
stopping at saving my soul but
seeking to stay in my heart as well.
Thank You for a wonderful life.
A life I will eternally live for You with
love, grace, and a pure heart.
Father, I am ever thankful.

Bird Song

Prayer Sight

You are like the sunshine
that shines upon the trees.
You are like the birds that fly
soaring through the breeze.

You make me see what I often miss
as You hold me in the air,
a realm of peace I've come to know
when I come to You in prayer.

You are My Life

Walking with You,
the deepest, brightest
desire of my whole being.
Like a burning fire,
flames reaching into the sky,
I long to sing by Your side.
My hand ever stayed in Yours,
I trust in You even when
I don't understand the
unfolding of Your plan.
You are the reason I live,
the reason I breathe each day.
You are why I try.
Why I pray
to be a blessing to others
because it pleases You.
Abba, please grant that I may
always long to go home to You
and walk steady in Your spirit.

Broken Wings

*Refiners fire and the heat of a tear
burns into the soul,
purifying what is found within and
leaving behind the mark of God.*

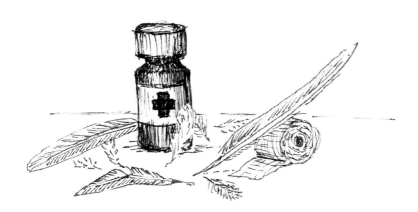

You are Invited

You sorrowful comforters,
your pity means little to me.
With sad eyes you gaze
upon my misfortune and
watch as I fall on my
knees to the ground.
You dare not enter into my
circle of tears but
stand outside with self-tied
hands feeling sorry for me.
You let me carry this burden alone,
the weight pulling me down
into the depths of a stormy sea.
But I have a rock I cling to,
a Savior who will rescue me
from my troubles.
He will guide me through the
thick darkness and bring me to the light.
He holds me fast in His hand and
won't let the waves overwhelm me.
I invite you to share this pain
and to know the Savior so when you too
are troubled and lost,
you'll have a road to lead you home.

Loneliness

Desolate and all alone against a stormy sea,
no one to confide in,
you ask who cares about me?
Don't let anyone in, there's nothing to gain,
'cause lonely hearts don't feel any pain.

You pray to God, He's the only one who hears,
your troubles, your sorrows,
no one else sees your tears.
You wonder where can I go, what have I done,
to deserve this despair, to be the only one?

You trust no one, be on your guard,
don't let down your wall,
you've worked too hard.
You might get hurt, you could fall fast,
everyone will hurt you, nothing will last.

Someday you will tell of the hurt that's inside,
but not today,
today in God you will hide.
You know God loves you, but others do too,
there's joy and hope just waiting for you.

Swallowed Pain

My heart aches with
sorrow and confusion.
Brimming with untold tears,
the pain is held prisoner within.
Clawing at the walls,
it cries out to be set free.
But that would be shameful
and it has nowhere to go.
So it stands there so alone
with loneliness and fear
threatening to swallow it down
the blackened hole of
hopelessness and despair.

Hidden Sights

You look into my eyes and see one who's
dreams have been torn at by the clawing night.
You see someone who is haunted by the
old path not followed, with the trees hanging down.
You don't see the hidden smiles amidst
the fog they dance in.
You don't see their hidden tears,
the calming vision to have a time of peace.
You see so much and yet so little,
yet I am afraid to let you
see me in my entirety.

Trust Persevering

I watched you wandering across the sea,
    wondering if there is more yet to be.
There are scars on your heart
    and blisters on your feet,
but there is a fire you still need to meet.

You've been let down by fellow man,
    but God is creating a higher made plan.
Learn the lessons presented,
    reflect on and know,
that God is caring for all above and below.

Keep reaching out to the people beside,
    and if they fail, in God you can hide.
For you need to keep trusting
    and love others too,
it's really your Savior caring through you.

Behind My Wall

I'm alone behind my wall.
Brick by brick, it's grown so high.
I won't let anyone in.
It's always a lie.
What will it take to tear down my wall?
If I leave, will I fall?
A friend and an enemy,
I'm a slave to the wall.
Can I break the chains?
Can I be free?
What is waiting beyond the wall for me?
Do I want to? Do I dare?
Is there anyone I can trust out there?
Who will help me?
Whom can I trust?
My master is with me, but friends are a must.
So I stand here, behind my wall,
wanting to leave, but afraid I will fall.

Wrenching Fire

Searing pain
wrenching sleep apart
  like bolts of lightening
   shooting across the sky.
   Twisting and burning
   limbs of trees and shrub,
setting ablaze the dark night
in heat and fire.
  Writhing in the bonds,
   crying in the agony.
   Then the storm passes and
        smoke drifts upward
              disturbing the view.

Battle Cry

Why do the nightmares come?
Why does life get turned upside down?
Why do we get tossed about
in the throws of an angry sea?
It's as if we are in a battlefield
fighting through the crimson swords
for the right to keep living.
And for what?
To tend to our wounds then run back again?
To sacrifice our lives to the cannons?
When shall the peace treaty be signed?
When can we at last go home to our fields?
Why does life happen as it does? Why? Why?
I don't have the answers,
I can only say glory be to God, thy will be done.

Learning to Fly

The Reader is You

Gold leaf sides
and scarlet cover
upon a table lies.
Rarely touched,
a layer of dust
shows its anguished cries.
A tale of rare beauty,
half is loved while
half remains unknown.
The reader hovers by,
praising the story yet
never knowing the plot,
loving the tale yet
touching it not.

To Trudge

Thirsty and tired,
I walk the road.
Weary and worn
I travel.
A lack of vision
only to match
my lack of rest,
stretches on ahead
while a forgotten past
lies dead behind.

Alone

All alone,
no one holds me, no one hugs me,
no one wipes away my tears.
I deal with my problems and feelings alone,
oh, so utterly alone!
No one cares when I go and when I come.
No one asks how my day went 'cause no one cares.
There are no shoulders to cry on
and no arms to wrap me in love.
I'm tired of being alone with no one to confide in.
I want someone who will always be there,
someone, somewhere.

Learning to Fly

A Sufferer's Prayer

I was once a dream and an imaginative spirit.
Soaring through the air, nothing could pull me down.
Then the shattering of illusions broke through.
Now I'm in the mud, mixed dirt and tears.
I'm still a dream outside, happy and free of care,
but inside I'm weeping a sufferer's prayer.
I cannot escape and I cannot die.
To live in this self-inflicted torture is death enough.
I don't know what to do and I'm scared.
I keep falling further down and
I don't know how to stop.
To crawl into a warm dark hole and
sleep this away would be sweet bliss.
Instead, I'm running an unending race,
wearing and worn.
Where does this end? Does it at all?
Or am I sentenced to this life of stress and
panic for all my days?
God, You are there, always beside me.
Please help me.
Be my hiding place from this world once more.
Give me the peace You have,
let it flow from Your love.
Be my guide, hold me to Your side,
and take me in Your arms.

Losing Light

There's a message on my heart
and it weighs upon my soul.
But now familiar sights have fallen by the road
and the night is closing in.
Strange creatures slide past me in the dark
as my feet stumble over land and sea.
My voice calls out to empty space.
No one is there to hear my haggard heart in
this forsaken and pitiless void.
I have a message to deliver
but I think I have lost my way.

Days Gone By

A smile remembered,
a touch embraced in heart.
Love once shared between two,
now the memory of one.
Empty arms aching for familiarity,
longing spirit without its friend.
Impassioned tears seeing
all that has been left behind
and all that has been lost long ago.
A flat image, the tattered remains
of a heavenly being on earth.
Past words voice the cold echo
through future ages to come.
But present is the pain,
the hurt of love no more.
Here is the tear that tells
the story of two once together,
now separate and apart,
forever wondering in grief
and hoping in love that what was
once two, and is now one,
will be two once again.

Between Friends

Since you were a small child,
I have watched over you.
I let you pull my tail
and drag me along like a blanket.
Always have I known when
you were anything less than happy,
even from a long ways away.
My fur has absorbed your tears
and my paws have held you.
I know you better than my own tail,
and I, more cherished than your hand.
Together we have laid in the dark,
sniffing the air, whiskers to cheek.
I've watched you fall asleep,
then moved down by your feet until morning.
You've dragged me out from under beds,
but I've always been the first one you wanted to see.
I've clawed at you when
I've been nervous or scared,
but you've loved every mark because it was mine.
We've been a sublime duet, you and I.
I've had a good life with you,
it's now time for you to let me go.
God has called me to Him,

to wait in Heaven until you join me there.
Death cannot part a love like ours.
God loves you so much more than I do,
and He will never leave.
Take comfort in Him Sarah,
the Lord cares for me too.
Trust me that the pain will lessen.
Although it may be hard, wipe the tears
and know I will always be with you.

Searching My Soul for You

I see your shadow before me,
outlined in silver wonder.
Like a cool mist on a cloudy day,
your spirit surrounds my body, echoing in my ears.
Expressions hang before my awareness,
reminding me of what is not there.
Empty hands caress my skin in solitude,
yearning to be real.
At night I lay in unrealized death,
tears racing from the open wound.
My arms hang limp in the air,
longing to feel your breath on my face.
Sympathetic smiles pass before my eyes,
begging assurance of my stability.
Questioning the existence of reality,
your voice whispers in my ear,
calming my searching soul.

Movements

How easily our worlds are shattered,
    how fast our safety falls,
how quickly illusions get battered,
    even as we hold onto the One who calls.
The assuredness of this life
    disappears beyond the sea
when what we've known is taken away
    and we are pushed back upon our knees.
But the things we thought were true
    are still movements in the night.
They are shadows upon the wall,
    they still move with dawn's first light.

Walking with the Dead

Old and broken down, cast aside with age,
forgotten names worn out and torn in two.
Crumbling and falling, tombstones that are no more.
Wandering through deserted lives,
I'm walking with the dead.
Dark silhouettes once were there,
fresh graves with consecrating tears.
Slowly, mournfully, they walk away,
never to be remembered again.
Endless rows of forgotten lives,
who will mourn you and who remembers?
Abandoned memories and dreams condemned,
no one is there to grieve over you anymore.
What were your lives and how did you die?
The innocent and guilty are lying side by side.
What is your story and what did you learn?
I'm frozen with despair when
I'm walking over the dead.
If you could rise, what would you say?
Cherish your friends and cherish your life,
it all too soon shall slip away.
I see children laughing and
old men dancing,
I leave once more, alive and free.
How many more shall pass away?
Lives torn apart,
hearts dashed on stone.
Tears fall from my eyes
as I think of the dead.
Soon I'll be gone, just like you.
Someone else will take my
place, and they too,
shall walk with the dead.

Broken Wings

Raggedy Ann and Andy

Raggedy Andy, a childhood dream.
But yarn red hair gets cut
and doll clothes get torn and stained.
The printed smile is faded to a frown
as dreams fall like clippings to the floor.
Ragged souls are separated
and Ann is gone.

Working in Me

Will my life count
for more than what I can see?
Is there a deeper laid plan
working in me?

Is my existence
a thread in the quilt?
Is my breath a rock
in the house God has built?

There are so many questions
I hope one day to find,
but glory be, I'll keep walking in faith
with Your love closely mine.

Caught

Caught in the fishing net
of daily life and lists of things to do,
as the struggle to breathe free
from sin and fear reels
in my mustard seed faith.
The hook of despair
tears at the mouth of my praise
and I cry out to You in
mournful tones.
Torn out of my true home,
I flop about the deck in failure
until with my last breath,
I quiet myself in You.
Lovingly You pick me up so tenderly,
holding me close to the water
and gently cradling me in Your hands.
Then firmly but in a compassionate way,
prying out of my life what has kept me from You,
and healing the scars it has left behind,
You free me into the deepest waters of joy
and I know deep inside that You will always
be the sole reason I swim through life and death,
ever thankful I was caught by You.

Forest of Broken Dreams

Beyond the farthest edge of earthly land,
across the endless coast of grain white sand,
there lies a forest few will find,
where fallen trees and
worn out dreams are left behind.
I walk along the path of reveries,
without aim, searching through the broken leaves.
A red one here, stained with blood,
a brown one there, caked with mud.
Upon the ground, these scattered lives,
where despair and lost hope always thrives.
But blowing wind, on its ever-changing course,
changing the has-beens by some unseen force.
Ever showing me new dreams to pursue,
I rise up once again, marked by the dew.

Learning to Fly

Flight Lessons

Flying above,
I share what I've learned,
praying that you
might share it in turn.

Letting Go

You have the gift,
it flows out from your heart,
don't be afraid to use it,
for you're God's work of art.

You have the fire,
it burns within your soul,
don't be afraid to let it out
and let it lose control.

You have the beauty,
it radiates from within,
don't be afraid to show it
and let your true self in.

You have the dream,
it's yearning for the chance,
don't be afraid to set it free,
lay back and watch it dance.

You have the love,
never stop from wanting more,
don't be afraid to let it flow
and let your spirit soar.

Flight Lessons

Rain

Rain runs down my face, cool and refreshing.
Eyes shut with upturned face, letting it come.
The gentle murmur fills my ears,
  whispering to my soul it's secrets of rejuvenation.
  Unlocking the frozen buds and hidden leaves,
  it penetrates the ground,
  bringing new life in its wake.
  Imagining myself part of the flow,
  invigorating the world,
  showering growth down upon the land
  and giving nourishment to those around it,
  I see what I could become,
  I could become the rain.

Shalom

Peace,
shalom,
is not the absence of conflict,
but the peace
within ourselves among
such conflict and tribulations.
It is the knowledge
in our hearts that
we have been bought by blood,
it is the knowledge of invulnerability
in the hands of a just
and merciful God.
And it is shalom that
He'll give us to the end.

The River Way

The river glides by, calm and peaceful.
Not knowing where it's going,
it flows on undisturbed.
Gently it slips past the thorns
and quietly carves out its path.
The waters don't rage and question.
They don't rebel against the way.
They simply accept the divine plan and
reflect the color of the sky.
Oh, why can I not be like the river?

Flying Lessons

The birds chirp from their boughs,
happy to be alive, happy to have wings.
They do not store for tomorrow or
slave away today in labor,
but sing their songs of love,
away from the world and
soaring in the open sky,
easing each other's burdens.
Boundaries do not matter and
food is all the same.
Unified they travel to an unknown end.
We should be like the birds for
together they go boldly to their God.

Sun Yearnings

The sun is always there.
Its rays warm my face as I turn
toward the nectar
pouring
from the sky for
I thirst for its
attention, for its retreat.
It does not care whom it shines upon
for it shines for all.
We all yearn to soak in its love,
to bask in its goodness.
What a happy day when we shall
yearn for God as we do for the sun.

Fly Free

When you open a clam,
there's a pearl inside.
When a caterpillar builds its cocoon,
it changes into a wonderful butterfly.
As when you ask the Lord into your heart,
you become beautiful.

A bird flying in the sky is carefree,
it does not worry about where it will sleep
or what it will eat at night.
It trusts the Lord to care for it.
Will not the Lord do the same for you?

The Savior hears each yearning voice,
He wraps us in His arms.
He will keep us safe from harm.
There is no mountain we can't climb,
no ocean we can't cross,
with Christ by our side.

The Lord is my Father and my friend.
He is my brother and a King.
He is the rock that I lean on
during times of joy and suffering.
I know He will always be there
because He loves me.

Challenging Faith

Sometimes God asks
for His children to do
a thing they don't like
to get them out of the pew.
But God knows what's best
for the children He loves,
and sometimes to follow
they need a soft shove.
So when they complain
about what's set before,
they cry out to God
and ask what's it for?
Then God replies,
"I understand all.
You see only a part
of this world great and tall.
When you don't see my plan,
trust me and see
the miracles wrought
to set you all free.
For I love you dearly
and I see all your pain,
your tears and your trials
and the struggling strain.
Just take my hand,
have faith and hold tight,
I'll give strength from above,
power and might."

The Gift of Time

I look forward to tomorrow
and relish today.
For the future holds many joys
and unknown dreams,
but the moment is here, happy and clear.
Yet in tomorrow are the things I cannot have today,
the things that inspire me, that I hold dear.
Yesterday, I did not know I would love today,
today was my future, the past was my moment.
I held the present in the palm of my hand,
gazed at it and thought about it.
I knew tomorrow would become today,
my moments would become my past.
What once was, I smile about,
what will be, are my dreams.
But what will be is ever changing.
Like the flowing of the tide,
tomorrow will never be known.
Today is what I have,
this moment is all I can hold on to.
What happens now shall too soon become the past.
What has been is a beautiful memory.
I look back on it and my heart is glad.
The yesterdays I have lived
have made me who I am today.
And for this, I am thankful.
Each day that passes is a gift,
each moment is precious.
So enjoy today, cherish the past,
and dream of tomorrow.

Beauty is as Beauty Does

A rose wrapped in dew welcoming the dawn.
A large ivory moon watching over the night.
Perhaps it may be a gentle flowing river
winding through emerald coated hills.
I have sought out these things and
see beauty yet they hold it not.
For the real beauty is in the soul.
With seeing eyes, looking around,
seeking out what is draped in glory.
Making what is beheld as beautiful
as what is found within.
To those around,
souls can shine like stars in the night.
You, dear one, have a beautiful soul
and a beast will never be.

Standing on Forever

Hope is eternal and
faith will carry you through.
Do not depend just on what
you can see and understand,
but stand on what you know
to be true. Stand on the
rock that has felt your
pain and holds you up.
For what is seen is passing
but faith in Him is forever.
Put your hope in Him my friend,
and He will carry you through.

Grace

Lord, I seek You above all things.
Your grace is sufficient for me
for though I may cry and call
my questions out to the heavens,
You have already given me hope of
life where I had only to die.
Were I to be alone with no love save Yours,
with no healthy being but Your broken body,
and nothing to claim but Your spirit,
I would still be joyfully content with Your grace.

Canyons

The pain is deep yet the
joy is deeper still.
For the more sorrow you bear,
the more love you can hold.
Anguish will carve out room
in your heart so you may know love.
Despair will etch into your bones
the canyons of bliss.

Learning to Fly

A Planet Full of Pain

There's not enough love,
there's too much hate.
Sometimes you wonder is it too late?
Can we solve our problems,
can we do it for sure?
Can we make our world
so it's nice, clean, and pure?
Racism and pollution,
it's poisoning our air.
Can we give it our love,
can we give it our care?
If you love our planet,
you need to do your part.
Give it your time,
give it your heart.
If we keep going this way,
what will we gain?
Because what we have here
is a planet full of pain.

God's Song

Believe in what your
heart is singing.
Though the notes are hard to hear,
I know it's God who's playing.

He's the one holding the flute,
and it's His hands caressing the keys
and though we may not understand it now,
it's still His song of peace.

The Song of the Saved

As time unfurls it's billowed sail,
over earth and sea, deathly pale.
Racing wind blows its force,
bringing life to a shattering course.
As the land swells up into a crown
and the seas pulse forward then through then down,
riding waves of endless sight,
going under into an endless night.
The moon's soft glow shall turn to blood
as flames sweep through the forest wood.
The sun will darken to partial beam,
while hell's black teeth shows brightest gleam.
Then on a day when all is lost,
they all will see how much pride cost.
The Lord will come and take away
those He loves on that last day.
To glory they'll go upon His breast,
beyond all evil for glorious rest.
Until that time when all shall see
Jesus is Lord and go down on bended knee,
His children will wait with peace in their hearts,
shining for God in their intermost parts.
Call on His name before you find it's too late.
Delight in His love and let go of your hate.
Go take your soul to the throne of the King,
then after earth dies, His melody sing.

Praise Sincere

I heard you singing praise to God,
but what is it you meant?
Have you really given your life to Him,
has He called you and you went?
Or are you sitting borderline,
between I don't, I do?
Are you truly singing praise to God,
or is it just for you?
Are you looking out for what you get
by being in this place?
Or are you eagerly anticipating
seeing glory in His face?
To ask ourselves these questions
is for us a vital part,
to know that we are in God's will
and He is in our hearts.

Miracles

Look for the miracles in your life,
the small events in your day
making all the difference
between death and life.
Search for their treasure
for the longer you reach,
the more you will you find.
God is working each day
both in big and little ways.
Cherish their beauty
and remember their blessings
for they can be His guidance
on your journey home.

Memories

Each memory is a treasure,
each one is a vital part
of the love you hold within yourself,
the tenderness out-flowing from your heart.

Sweet memories can hold warmth
and cold ones can hold tears,
but each is a lesson learned
to help you through the years.

Remembering God's power,
the past through holy eyes,
you will see it as an eternal flame
and in your soul internalize.

Wrap them tight into your thoughts
but remember that you're here,
using what you've come to know
to bring a smile near.

For they are what will encourage you,
these lights upon the sea,
they are what will let you know
that God is there and loving thee.

Shine On

Like the bright morning sun,
you can shine upon those around you.
Lighting up their lives with your smiles
and words of encouragement,
you can cast rays of sunshine
into the gloom of a darkened world.
You people who do this,
may you be blessed in God's sight.
May your lives illuminate and strengthen
the ones who flock to hear you,
the ones who find joy in being around you and
who see in you, the face of God.
For it is in your lives that unbeknownst to you,
His children will find Him and it is in you
He will uplift and uphold them.
So shine on children of the King,
shine like the sun for the lost will seek you out and
the lonely will find companionship and peace.
Shine on lovers of the Lord, for it is in you He
will light the way for His children to come home.

Learning to Fly

Playing
in the Wind

*Dancing upon the wild wind
among the shining stars,
imagining what could be
when we let ourselves dream.*

The Great Pirate Lissa

There once was a girl called Lissa,
who sailed the raging sea.
With a terribly fine ship,
a mighty fine pirate was she.

To far-off lands she set her quest,
to find adventure she would scheme.
So to the moon she went with sword in hand
and in eye a sparkling gleam.

With a laugh and a swagger
she departed the ship.
"Blow de' man down!"
she liked to quip.

With a purpose in her step,
'twas the moonbeam she sought.
Just how to get it
was her only thought.

She swanked over volcanoes
and fought every foe,
walked along the Sea of Dreams,
and climbed the crater Tycho.

A dark shadow rose ahead
and looked her in the eye.
Said the woollylillyum,
"For the moonbeam, me you must get by."

The Great Pirate Lissa stood unmoved,
matched his gaze and drew her sword.
With a wry smile she turned and said,
"Even from you, I'll get my reward."

She thrust to the left
and he sank to the right.
The battle was long,
they didn't finish till night.

"You have fought well
and have strength it is true,
but to find what you seek,
answer me this about you."

Lissa was rather surprised,
but with great bravery yet.
The woollylillyum leaned over and said,
"In the life of a pirate, what is the best to be met?"

The Great Pirate Lissa
thought long and hard
of swords and daggers,
patches and guards.

But one thing was missing,
she studied and knew.
A pirate must have courage
and a constant good character too.

She answered him thus
and he smiled and said,
"Good answer brave pirate,
to the moonbeam we'll tread."

They walked for a mile,
and in a cave they did go.
In the back lay a chest,
within: a moonbeam aglow.

He handed it to her
and with a woollylillyum smile,
said to the Great Pirate Lissa,
"I'm glad you found your treasure, it's worth every trial."

Together they swaggered
all the way back to the ship.
As she walked up the plank she turned
and said, "Thanks for the tip."

She went to the head,
her moon adventure was done.
Maneuvered the wheel
and turned the keel towards the sun.

If you ever meet a girl with moonbeam in tow,
with a swank in her step and a shining charisma,
know that you meet one of the best in the world,
the Great Pirate Lissa.

Living Dreams

High upon the window sill,
    upon the world where dreams stand still,
looking out unto the sea,
    where birds do soar and souls fly free.
Ivy climbs and towers rise,
    over sea, endless skies.
Diamonds shining in the night,
    music flowing, giving light.
Here I stand and here I sing
    of you and me living dreams.

In the Master's Hand

The shadow of words, an echoing voice,
a presence surrounding you.
To be the unknown force, the soul toucher.
To be the box holding the pearl,
the spirit writing the words.
In that is the joy,
to be the quiet tool in the Master's hand.
Tears and touched hearts are more than a reaction,
they are a forever legacy
for the unknown artist of words.
The lover of life in the fog
writing in hope of the dream
a work might stand on it's own.
And when the dawn comes
and dreams are realized,
the author walks back into the shadows,
deeply moved but perfectly content
in just being the tool in the Master's hand.

Nevermore in College

By Sarah K. Hoggatt and Kathryn Magura

Students entered in, the teacher droned on.
"Shalt thou ever give us rest from tiresome words?"
The teacher candidly replied, "Nevermore."

Students asked thy teacher,
"Shalt thou ever be interesting?"
Quothed he, "Nevermore!"

"Shalt thee ever not fade away?"
"Nevermore, you do as I say!"
"Shalt thee ever not stutter?"
"Um, um, nevermore, um."

"Shalt thou ever change tone of voice?
To go from high to low is sweet music in my ear,
and thee art a clashing symbol, never ceasing."
He answered, "Nevermore!"

His students grew weary, took notes in a dreary.
One cried, "Please sir, can we leave?"
To which he replied, "Nevermore, you dweeb!"

Students cried and wept bitter tears,
"Shalt we ever see the light of day?"
To which the teacher screamed,
"Nevermore, here you shall stay!"

The students revolted, and one yelled,
"We'll get you fired!"
"Not so my simpleton student," replied he,
"for you are very tired."
To which they all fell fast asleep and with a snore,
the teacher whispered one final victorious, "Nevermore."

Playing in the Wind

Midterm Blues

I woke up late this morning, falling out of bed.
Third week of school, with a mid-term right ahead.
Didn't feel like studying, gonna do bad anyway.
Never picked up the book,
day-dreaming my life away.
Ignored the loud alarm,
gonna trash that clock today.
Got the wrong building, the mid-term is which way?
I'm guessing all the answers,
I'm playing tic-tac-toe.
I hate this class, don't care what I got anymore.
Got the test back this morning, wasn't very fun.
Flunked it pretty badly, I'm just so glad I'm done.
I'll try and study next time, won't get behind again.
I got the mid-term blues, I got the mid-term blues.

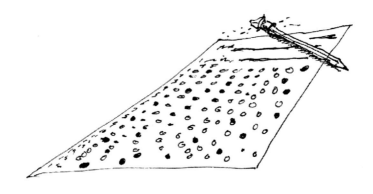

Learning to Fly

Urquhart Castle

I remember
the day I was built.
Cautious hands laying my stones and
how my Lord flew his scarlet colors.
The celebration of my birth and
how couples whirled joyfully across my floor.
The sound of horse hooves
trotting across my wooden bridge
to the sound of silver trumpets.

I remember
the day the attack came.
My thick walls kept those who
depended on me safe from harm.
But then came an attack I could not defend.
Time swelled in, rushing over me as
violet clouds billowed in the wake of a storm
taking away those that I knew.
In my tower now, no maiden stands.
No gallant knight with lance comes in.
Where music once flowed comes empty wind.
I am from another time, useless here.

But wait...
Someone again has entered beneath my roof,
someone again wanders through my rooms.
They stand on the battlements where my
scarlet banners once flew.
They look out my windows over the valley and
they remember.

Eternal Tides

Everlasting sky flows from above
as I dance through the stream
beside your seeking spirit.
Singing waters tune our hearts
to forever melodies of time as
living winds lift our longing souls
into outstretched arms of eternity.
Intertwined fingers are grasped
by a tender God who
longs to touch His children.
As we turn around in our twirling games,
we are taken up into the clouds beside Him.
Searching the eyes of our Abba King,
running with the waves beyond the sea,
we fall into a convergent mist of wonder,
back to ourselves and the ever-flowing tide.

Draw Me In

Where did you go oh my soul?
Where have you wandered
in the far off ridges of green?
If I called you, unlocked the door,
if I decreed you no judgment,
just empty space–deep and near,
if I welcomed you, breathed your breath,
would you have music to sing?
Approach the stairs, take the climb,
make your space, draw me in,
speak in words so I can hear.
Oh my soul.

Magic Carpet

Looking up,
seeing the air around me out of control.
The wind whistling in my ears
and a magic carpet appearing beneath me.
Being aware the air is following my movements,
standing on the carpet,
arms outstretched, moving in a circle,
feeling the wind follow my fingertips.
Jumping into the breeze,
sensing it gently letting me down.
Soon dancing with wild abandon,
following, leading, moving, holding me.
The carpet lifting me up into the stars,
flinging me upward, laughing, like a teddy bear.
Twisting my body around and
falling back into the safe arms of God.

Blackberries

Blackberries hanging
among the thorns,
awaiting exhilarated
young hands to weave
through the vines,
picking the delectable treats,
wrapping them in
pillows of dough,
folded, wrapped up tight
in silvery orbs of awaited delight.
Cast into the flames,
brought into fruition
as the sun runs through the blue.
Eyes watch the flames until at last!
The silvery orbs are removed…
    and opened…
        Sweet bliss of YUM!

Icebergs

Icebergs float upon the sea
where we sit and enjoy our tea.
Dolphins laughing swim on by,
as the moon soars in the sky.
Stars ablaze alight the night,
giving guidance, giving sight.
A magic place, a place to BE,
this place of joy,
this place to be free.

Hide and Go Seek with God

One day, near the end of the week,
I asked God if He'd like to play hide and go seek.
He smiled at me and said that He would,
so we joined our hands and hiked to the wood.
Looking at me, He said I was it,
I started to count and on a stump I did sit.
God hurried away and in a place He did hide,
I got up and looked, to find Him I tried.
But God's a good hider, you shall soon see,
for it took me hours to find Him,
in fact, it took three.
I checked behind trees, in a small cave I did go,
looked in the stream, but with nothing to show.
I could hear the Lord laughing,
I knew not where from,
but His echoing voice called out to me, "Come".
I asked Him, "Oh where?" for I wanted to share
this place He had found, what seemed like thin air.
He said close your eyes and follow your heart,
for then you will find Me and our true adventure will start.
I couldn't help but smile so I closed my eyes,
walked through the grass and felt the ground rise.
I thought He was there so I ran up the hill,
opened my eyes but didn't see Him yet still.
I let out a sigh, and turned back around,
saw Him standing there, but He didn't make a sound!
With amazement I asked Him where He had hid,
He said the place He liked best, is where He was led.
I wondered where could that be
in all the world that He made?
He told me where He had been,
is where He had stayed.

The place He liked best, was right by my side,
so not wanting to leave, that's where He did hide.
It was my turn to hide, so in a ravine I did go,
covered in bushes and crouched really low.
God called my name, looked everywhere,
walked through the wood
and searched with great care.
But He knew where I was
the whole length of time,
for soon He came over and
down the ravine He did climb.
He gave me a bear hug
with a twinkle in His eye,
but then we looked up and
noticed night had come nigh.
Together we left, hide and go seek was now done,
walked to the cliff, to watch the red sun.
As it sank down below, into its own little bag,
I thought, to keep an eye on God, tomorrow it's tag.

Learning to Fly

Liftoff

Raising wings into the blue expanse,
A new beginning to life
and a new perspective on living.

Words of the Father

I know you're depressed, you think there's no light,
you're trapped in the darkness,
in the cold, lonely night.
There's nothing for you, there's nowhere to go,
your heart is aching and you feel desperately low.

You're longing to leave the world and its kind,
climbed into your hole, to leave your life behind.
But holes are darker than the world out there,
out in the world,
there are people who love you and care.

I know you're tempted to let your life pass you by,
feeling so worthless, you can't even cry.
You won't share your pain, you don't let anyone see,
no one to confide in, not even Me.

I'm longing to hold you and walk on the way,
hoping your trouble upon Me you'll lay.
Living in Me you can shine upon lives,
don't let your dreams
get lost in the strife.

So please come on out,
trust Me and see,
the things you can do,
the beautiful person you are
and will be.
Your passion for Me
will never lead you astray,
don't be discouraged,
every day's a new day.

Forever Loved

I stumble toward You,
drained and empty of strength.
You pick me up into Your arms
and settle me down in Your love.
Safe in Your protection,
I lay down my heavy head
as You cover me with Your hands.
You are my comfort and my joy.
In You, I will be forever loved.

Fear No Evil

Memories are before my eyes,
my body shakes and I am defenseless.
God steps up beside me,
He takes my hand and holds me in His arms.
"No one can hurt you anymore my child.
No one can come near you.
I will protect you,
you are safe and secure and
no longer have to be afraid.
Be bold in Me, fear no evil,
for evil will now fear you."

Moonlight

Brightly shining within the darkness,
the moon casts its glow upon the still night.
Its radiant light shows the
way to weary travelers,
providing strength giving brightness
full of comfort, truth, and hope.
In its shadow lies a sanctuary
from the terrors of the night,
a haven from the dark
midnight surrounding the world.
Within its view is an ever deepening
joy coursing through the desert,
and thoughts of its presence buoys
up life upon the empty and unknown sea.
Thank God for the moon for it reflects His
love onto the earth and
into the hearts and lives of many.
May I always seek it out and
belong within its sphere.

Spring

For you the winter is past.
The rain is gone and the
clouds are clearing.
The tears you cried will be
washed away in the bright
sunshine of spring and the
darkness you've borne
will be flooded with light.
Have you not seen the daffodils
shining brightly with color?
Have you not heard the birds
singing in their boughs?
They are heralding a new dawn.
Look, it is upon you!
It is a new beginning,
fresh with wonder and love.
Rise up, cast off the cloak
of weariness and frustration
and instead clothe yourself
in all the glory of spring
and the new life it will bring.

New Life

Abba, You delight to cut my pain and
take up the filth in which I have lain.
I am no longer held within their grasp,
with all the titans of my past.
The wind blew hard and the thunder rolled
but now Your child You uphold.
Your power strong and mighty grasp,
my broken heart You now enclasp.
You make me forget what I've been through,
You've healed my life and made me new.
I am blessed with joy while loved in Your sight,
protected from the terrors of night.
The new dawn is come and light is here,
You've picked me up and held me near.
You take my hand, their vengeance I shed,
and away from their hurtful touches I'm lead.
I am the new blade that riseth green and
I am the flowers blooming in spring.
Rain comes and washes the old ways away,
as I've been brought into Your love this day.
Thank You Lord for giving me life and
for taking me away from all the old strife.
For You I will stand and for You I will sing
and then to Heaven I'll go where Your glory will ring.

Open Doors

Don't tell me of anger or hatred.
I want nothing to do with the
dark sludge you choose to wallow in.
Don't invite me in to dwell
in darkness with you for I will not go.
I will not let my life be controlled by
events of the past as you choose to be.
To validate yourself with the pain
others have inflicted upon you
is a useless and never ending trial.
I won't sit beside you as you sing
the words but refuse to live them.
I won't stand idly by making polite
conversation while constantly
worrying about how you'll take
what I say, how you will proclaim
how much you are hurt and watch
you cling to your pain like a
child who knows no love.
I refuse to deny who I am for
who you want me to be.
I won't take the guilt and shame
you want to put me with.
I won't be blamed for your feelings.
You are like a prisoner who refuses
to let go of their chains after
being set free from their cold cell.
The door has been opened,
don't you see it swinging wide?
Joy and healing could be yours to keep
but you sit wailing at the damp,
complaining how your freedom

has been ripped up and taken away.
I will not stay here with you
for I see my chance to be set free.
I know now that I can go out and truly
live a life filled with love and acceptance.
A life that is not ruled by past
pain but by trust and truth.
I will not sacrifice my light heart
for your heavy burdens.
You have a choice to carry them
but you cannot make me do so.
I wish you knew what it felt like to be free.
For I know if you did,
you would leave your baggage behind and
enter into this world of contentment and peace.
There is nothing better, nothing sweeter.
Aren't you tired of being bitter?
Doesn't your heart yearn for
healing and completeness?
I know mine sure did.
My heart was broken and sore.
I always had to watch myself,
thinking I had to prove I was worthy of love.
My feet were bleeding after walking on
egg shells for so long.
I believed people would stop loving me
if I missed a step or said something wrong.
I thought I could lose it all and
was so taken up with keeping it all together
I never got to just be God's child, beloved.
But God has taken my hand in His and
He cut all the weights that I ever knew.
He walked up to me, took me in His arms
and held me close to His heart.
He taught me I was loved no matter what.

Liftoff

That I was loved by His children.
He gave me real joy, real peace.
He gave me healing and freedom.
Crying is no longer a shame but the
cleansing tide of love.
A tide that goes beyond your thinking
and instead of tearing apart,
it builds many together, one heart in unity.
People see it and wonder,
and I yearn to do the same for them,
but I know only they can walk the path to God.
It's a path full of hard steps, and
I know it's difficult to let go of what
you have held onto for so very long.
But the Lord longs to do it for you.
He is anxiously awaiting for you to stop clutching
your pain so He can fill you with
serenity and blessed assurance of His love.
I pray someday you will understand
what I have been gifted with and how it's
unalterably changed me and how I live my life.
It's a complete change, a new birth to living.
I can no longer return to the weighty chains
of darkness and of self-reprobation.
Instead I rejoice, falling to my knees at
God's goodness in giving me such a
new and beautiful heart, a beautiful life.
I have walked out the prison door
and I will never enter it again.
Don't you want freedom too?
Doesn't your heart long to rise on eagle's wings?
It can be yours, but it's your choice.
I've made mine, what will yours be?

Dreams Come True

A heart without a home
and a spirit without a dwelling place.
Hovering over the vast open sea
with no place to rest a soul.
Broken and covered in disappointment,
lonely and examining its existence.
Raggedly tired, it wanders about.
Down the road it trods,
a self flowing with questions,
searching for so many answers.
Unknown even to itself,
in a quest for healing and love.
Entering into the archway it comes,
awkward and clumsy it seems.
In a quiet corner sitting still,
then venturing out into discovery.
With cautious steps coming forward,
looking about with curious eyes.
A friendly hand reached out,
a kind smile shared by another
helps overcome nervousness and
encourages ideas to be shared.
Like coming to a pool of cool water,
finding the embracing tenderness
of an old world in the dawn of morning.
A familiar echo vibrates through the walls
with a new harmony blending into the tune.
A corner is turned, a new birth has begun,
and the spirit discovers a love to be born.
Stone by stone, a new home is built,
cared for by new relations, new hearts.
A tie is bound, a rope is braided into a web of compassion

and tender touches.
Wrapped in safety,
a soul discovers itself and its worth,
opening to dreams and warmth.
Hope replaces despair and
a rock replaces the drift in a raging sea.
A clasp is gripped and weights start to fall
into a land of no return.
Healing transforms the dance into
one of joy, peace, and gladness.
Bright lights line the path of
the eagle soaring to new heights,
leaving behind the old ways.
Flying into new territory and
challenging what could be,
it joins the procession and
takes part in the circle of fellowship.
Laughter surrounds it,
faces shine as the sun
and light chases out the dreary darkness,
the glow warming the coldest of days.
Comfort holds it close,
and undeserved grace abounds about.
Donning a robe of servitude,
it quietly goes about its work,
trying to return the unspeakable gift
it has so beautifully received.
Knees bent and tears falling,
crying out thanks to the Father
for making such dreams of depth,
such a love of life,
and such amazing people
walk out of visions of fancy,
enter into reality, and come true.

My Dawn is in You

Soft silent word,
the wink of an eye,
tender touch of a friend
to bring the dawn nigh.
Light-filled lifting voice,
vast fields to explore,
a flower in bloom
and a love to live for.
New bird out of shell,
bright blade rising green,
the melting of snow
show things never seen.
Fresh breath of life,
a joy deeply known,
bright song in the heart
to sing of one's own.
Mystical morning,
the sun shining through.
What a glorious day
when my dawn is in You.

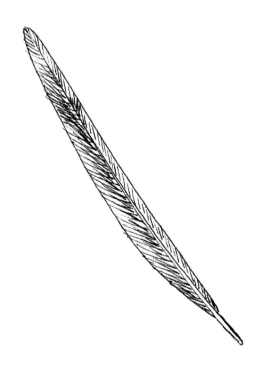

Epilogue: Learning to Fly

I've come to sit at His feet,
His voice whispering in my ear,
trying to catch a faint glimpse of the King
standing beside me here.
And I have come to love Him,
He is my life, my all,
my comfort and my delight,
for I have heard Him call.
So I will humbly follow
wherever He may lead,
knowing even darker times
are exactly what I need.
'Cause it is through the trials
I learn lessons from above,
the things God wants me to know
like joy and peace and love.
So as we are sailing through the sky,
soaring in His hands,
I am passing along what I've learned
so you might understand.
I'm wanting you to know
what this all has meant to me,
the journey of my life,
and the Lord who set me free.
I pray you will be blessed
and that His holy light will shine,
that you will take His hand
and in His heart entwine.
For I have come to know
nothing can compare
to the wild love He gives to you
out in the open air.

About the Author and Illustrator

Sarah Katreen Hoggatt, the author, has been writing creatively for over nineteen years and loves the idea of painting art by using words. She is a freelance writer, speaker, editor, visual artist, and spiritual director with a passion for ministering to searching souls. She holds a Master of Arts degree in Christian Ministry and a Certificate of Spiritual Formation and Discipleship from George Fox Evangelical Seminary in addition to her Bachelor of Science degree from Oregon State University. Sarah currently makes her home in Salem, Oregon where she enjoys the theatre, photography, hiking, and creating things with her hands. She is passionate about living her life as a gift.

Richard McConochie, the illustrator, is an Oregon native who wouldn't have it any other way. He holds a Bachelor of Science in Philosophy from Oregon State University, where he met the author, and a Masters of Architecture from the University of Oregon. He is inspired by the subtlety of nature and the strength of the human heart. One day, he hopes to teach art and dance to a new generation of dreamers. "It is not enough to question the students—you will only make them think of answers. Give them the answer, then make them question it."